WORLD MYTHOLOGIES

MYTHS OF THE ANCIENT GREEKS

Pliny O'Brian

Cavendish Square
New York

Published in 2016 by Cavendish Square Publishing, LLC
243 5th Avenue, Suite 136, New York, NY 10016

First Edition

Library of Congress Cataloging-in-Publication Data

O'Brian, Pliny, author.
Myths of the ancient Greeks / Pliny O'Brian.
pages cm. — (World mythologies)
Includes bibliographical references and index.
ISBN 978-1-5026-0988-5 (hardcover) ISBN 978-1-5026-0989-2 (ebook)
1. Mythology, Greek. 2. Greece—Religion. I. Title.

BL783.O27 2016
292.1'3—dc23
2015025194

Editorial Director: David McNamara
Editor: Amy Hayes
Copy Editor: Rebecca Rohan
Art Director: Jeffery Talbot
Designer: Joseph Macri
Senior Production Manager: Jennifer Ryder-Talbot
Production Editor: Renni Johnson
Photo Research: J8 Media

The photographs in this book are used by permission and through the courtesy of: Prisma/UIG/Getty Images, front, back cover and 1; Gian Lorenzo Bernini (Italian, 1598–1680) and students (Jastrow (2006)) [Public domain], File: Medusa Bernini Musei Capitolini.jpg via Wikimedia Commons, 4; Unknown artist, (Jastrow (2006) [Public domain], File: Zeus Otricoli Pio-Clementino Inv257.jpg via Wikimedia Commons, 7; Universal History Archive/UIG via Getty Images, 8-9; G. Nimatallah/De Agostini/Getty Images, 10, 13; French School, 19th century/Private Collection/© Look and Learn/Bridgeman Images, 16; Giuseppe Collignon (Italian, 1778 - 1863) (Unknown) [Public domain], File: Giuseppe Collignon - Prometheus Steals Fire from Apollo's Sun Chariot, 1814.jpg via Wikimedia Commons, 19; After Myron [CC BY-SA 4.0 (http://creativecommons.org/licenses/by-sa/4.0)], File: Discobolus in National Roman Museum Palazzo Massimo alle Terme.jpg via Wikimedia Commons, 22; Louis de Silvestre [Public domain], File:Louis de Silvestre Deckengemaelde Zwinger.jpg via Wikimedia Commons, 26-27; Soerfm (Own work) [CC BY-SA 3.0 (http://creativecommons.org/licenses/by-sa/3.0)], File: Francisco de Goya, Saturno devorando a su hijo (1819-1823) crop.jpg via Wikimedia Commons, 28; © Rolf Krahl/[CC BY-SA 3.0 de (http://creativecommons.org/licenses/by-sa/3.0/de/deed.en)], File: Barockgarten Großsedlitz - Rhea.jpg via Wikimedia Commons, 32; Plaque Campana, Dance of the Curetes, from Myrina, Asia Minor (terracotta) (b/w photo), Greek/Louvre, Paris, France/Alinari/Bridgeman Images, 34; Jan Cossiers [Public domain], File: Jan Cossiers - Prometeo trayendo el fuego, 1637.jpg via Wikimedia Commons, 36; Etruscan/Getty Images, 39; Ann Ronan Pictures/Print Collector/Getty Images, 42; Greek, 5th Century/Louvre, Paris, France/Peter Willi/Bridgeman Images, 44; Walter Crane/Private Collection/ Photo © Christie's Images/Bridgeman Images, 47; Evelyn De Morgan(1855-1919)/© The De Morgan Centre, London / Bridgeman Images, 50; Fine Art Images/Heritage Images/Getty Images, 53; © Marie-Lan Nguyen/Wikimedia Commons, File: Tondo Minotaur London E4 MAN.jpg via Wikimedia Commons, 55; Peter Paul Rubens/(1577-1640) (attr. to)/Private Collection/Bridgeman Images, 59; Unknown, Marie-Lan Nguyen (User: Jastrow), 2007, British Museum [Public domain], File: Theseus Minotaur BM Vase E84.jpg via Wikimedia Commons, 63; Anthony van Dyck [Public domain], File: Anthony van Dyck - Daedalus and Icarus - Google Art Project.jpg via Wikimedia Commons, 65; Roman/Museo Torlonia, Rome, Italy/Alinari/Bridgeman Images, 68; By Jacob Peter Gowy [Public domain], File: Gowy-icaro-prado.jpg via Wikimedia Commons, 70; Superstock, 72; Daderot/File:The Judgment of Paris by the Master of the Argonaut Panels, c. 1480, Italian, tempera on panel, detail - Fogg Art Museum - DSC02379.JPG/Wikimedia Commons, 77; Antonio Canova [CC BY 2.5 (http://creativecommons.org/licenses/by/2.5)], File: Helen Canova VandA A.46-1930.jpg via Wikimedia Commons, 81.

Printed in the United States of America

TABLE OF CONTENTS

INTRODUCTION

The Importance of Mythology

Medusa is a terrible monster of Greek mythology. She was said to have a head full of snakes.

Fom folk heroes to gods, campfires to cathedrals, **myths** are stories that are told over and over again. These important stories deepen the identity and customs of a culture. Myths shaped the lives of the people who heard them. These timeless tales of a civilization's gods and heroes were a part of the beliefs, values, and practices of people who lived long ago.

What makes a story a myth? Unlike a narrative written by a particular author, a myth is a traditional story that has been handed down from generation to generation, first orally and later in written form. Nearly all myths tell the deeds of gods, goddesses, and other divine beings. These age-old tales were once widely accepted as true and sacred. Their primary purpose was to explain the mysteries of life and the origins of a society's customs, institutions, and religious rituals.

Mythology (the whole collection of myths belonging to a society) played an important role in ancient cultures. In very early times, people created myths to explain the awe-inspiring, uncontrollable forces of nature, such as thunder, lightning, darkness, drought, and death. Even after philosophers and scientists began to develop more rational explanations for these mysteries, myths continued to provide comforting answers to the many questions that could never be fully solved. People of all cultures have asked the same basic questions about the world around them, such as how did the world begin, what is the purpose of living, and what happens after death?

The myths of ancient Greece are often funny, strange, and full of adventure. There is trickery, wisdom, and folly. These myths were not just created out of people's imaginations. A civilization's geography, government, and culture all influence what stories are told, and which stories eventually become myth. For example, one of Greece's most beloved heroes was Theseus, who killed the Minotaur. Theseus was loved as a mythic hero who is credited with setting up democracy in Greece. Whether or not Theseus was real, democracy certainly was, and his myth lived on as legacy.

Mythology serves as instruction, inspiration, and entertainment. Well-known stories offer people in a society a way to express their fundamental beliefs and values and communicate these beliefs to future generations. Myths preserve and embellish tales of a civilization's accomplishments and teach important lessons about conduct and priorities. These captivating stories provided enjoyment to countless listeners and readers in ancient times, just as they do today.

This bust is one artist's interpretation of the most powerful god in Greek mythology, Zeus.

WORLD MYTHOLOGIES

MYTHS OF THE ANCIENT GREEKS

PART 1: Who Were the Greeks?

The Land and Sea of Greece

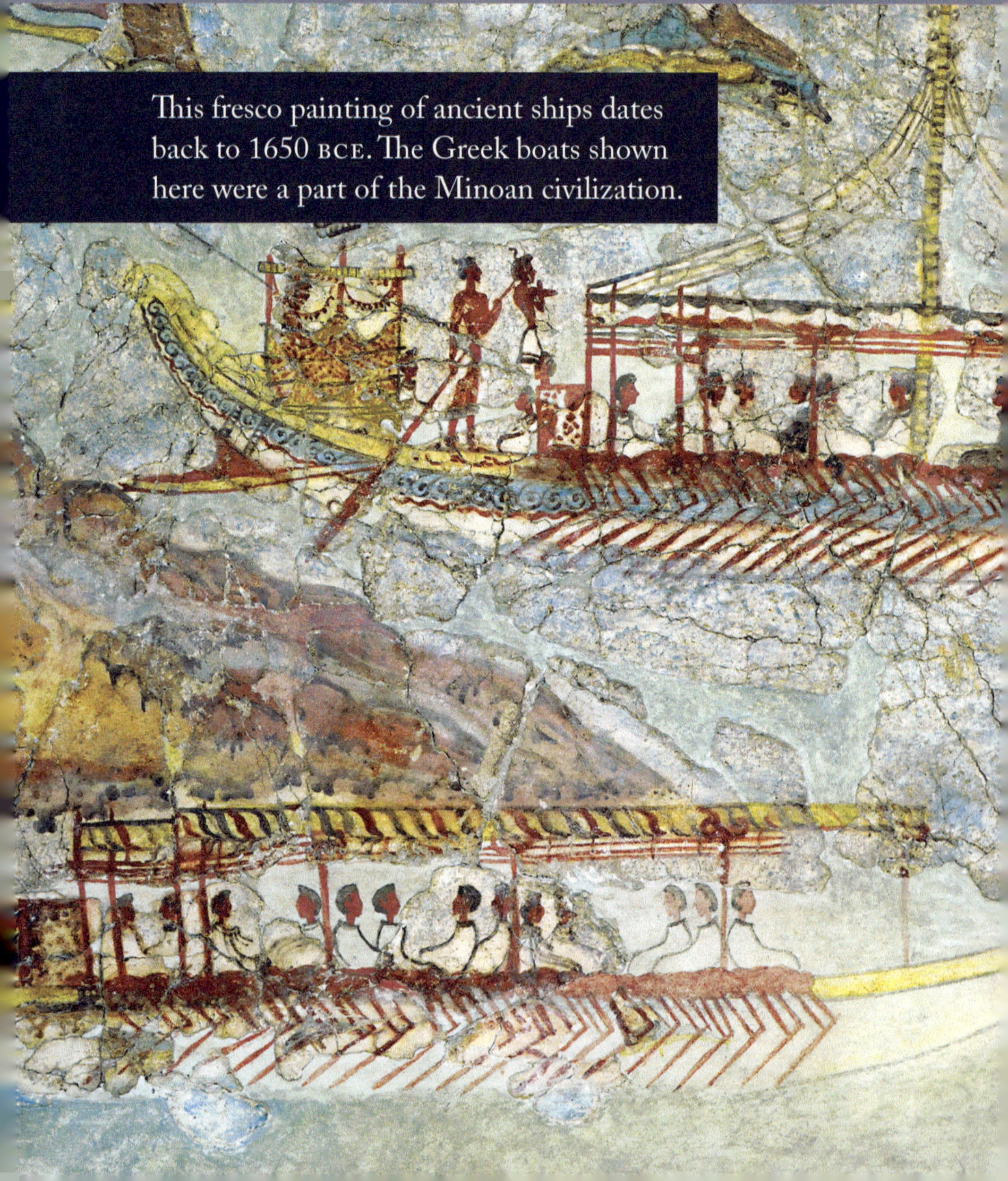

This fresco painting of ancient ships dates back to 1650 BCE. The Greek boats shown here were a part of the Minoan civilization.

The country of Greece is on the Balkan Peninsula and includes many nearby islands. The ancient Greeks made Greece their home, as well as other lands in southeastern Europe, around the Aegean Sea. These famous seafarers established settlements across a broad area. They spread north and east to the Black Sea and Asia Minor (present-day Turkey), west to parts of Italy and Sicily, and south to the coast of Africa.

The landscape of mainland Greece is rugged and mountainous. Only about a quarter of the rocky countryside is suitable for farming. Because of the shortage of natural resources, the people of this region have always depended heavily on the sea. Since ancient times, the Greeks have fished in the coastal waters and sailed the seas to trade with settlements on close-lying islands and distant shores.

The natural environment helped shape the stories told by the people of ancient Greece. Many of the Greek myths were set against a background of mountains, caves, and seas. The mountains of mythology were wild, mysterious places where divine beings roamed. Most sacred of all was Mount Olympus, Greece's highest peak, whose snow-capped crown held the palaces of the great Olympian gods. Mountain caves might be the birthplace of a god or the lair of a savage beast. The myth "The Beginning of All" on page 28 describes the birth of Zeus, king of the Olympians, in a cave on the island of Crete.

The Greeks also believed that the sea was home to many different **deities**, monsters, and mythical creatures.

The most powerful god of the sea was Poseidon. If Poseidon was happy, the seas were calm, but if he was not, his anger would bring crashing waves and terrible storms. Many an ancient sailor sacrificed bulls and other offerings to stay in this god's favor.

PART 1: Who Were the Greeks?

A Long and Revered History

This is a Minoan sculpture of a bull's head. Bulls were an important symbol in Greek mythology.

Greek myths were influenced by the history and politics of the time. The first great civilization of ancient Greece emerged on the island of Crete, around 3000 BCE. It became known as **Minoan**, after its mythical founder, King Minos. According to one myth, Minos's father was Zeus, the head of the gods on Mount Olympus. The king's magnificent palace in the city of Knossos was the setting for several myths, including "The Hero Theseus and the Minotaur," and "The Tragedy of Daedalus and Icarus."

While the Minoans flourished on Crete, another civilization was developing on the Greek mainland, centered in the ancient city of Mycenae. The warlike people of the **Mycenaean** civilization lived in huge fortress-cities ruled by powerful kings. Around 1400 BCE the Minoan civilization declined, and the Mycenaeans became the dominant power on Crete. As the cultures of these two great civilizations mingled, the Minoans' ancient stories of gods and other supernatural beings found new life in Mycenaean tales.

In time, the Mycenaean civilization also faded. Some historians think that the decline was caused by foreign invasions, while others believe that Mycenaean society was torn apart by conflicts among its warrior kings. Whatever the cause, Greece entered a long period of upheaval known as the Dark Age. Throughout these troubled times, the ancient Minoan-Mycenaean tales were preserved through the poetry and songs of wandering **minstrels**.

Around 800 BCE, a new Greece emerged, made up of many small mainland and island communities.

The people of these scattered settlements developed an alphabet and began to write down their ancient tales in imaginative histories called **epic** poems. The first of the Greek epics were the *Iliad* and the *Odyssey* by Homer. These famous poems describe events surrounding the Trojan War, a great conflict between the Mycenaean Greeks and the ancient city of Troy. Parts of the long tale of the Trojan War are retold on page 72.

In the fifth century BCE, Greece entered an era of wealth, power, and accomplishment often called the Golden Age. Hundreds of Greek **city-states**, or poleis, had been established across the Mediterranean world. Each **polis** had its own independent government and traditions. While the people of the Greek city-states were politically divided, they all shared the same basic language, along with many of the same religious beliefs and myths.

The Golden Age came to an end in 338 BCE, when Philip II, king of **Macedonia**, conquered the Greek city-states. Under Philip's leadership, the independent poleis joined together in a united federation. Philip's son, Alexander the Great, led that federation in a ten-year military campaign, building the largest empire the world had ever known. Wherever his armies claimed victory, from Egypt to India to Afghanistan, Alexander founded cities modeled on the Greek city-states.

When Alexander the Great died in 323 BCE, the power of Greece faded away. In its place rose the mighty Roman Empire. The Romans admired and imitated Greek culture. They kept alive many of the traditions, beliefs, art, and mythology of ancient Greece. As Rome expanded, Greece's cultural influence spread throughout their vast empire.

PART 1: Who Were the Greeks?

Democracy and Society

Men decide on laws in the Assembly of Athens.

At different times and places, the Greek people were ruled by chiefs, **tyrants**, groups of nobles, and kings. Governments changed many times. Kingdoms rose and fell, and city-states formed. The world's first democracies were created in Greece. Athens was the strongest and most democratic city-state. Many other Greek city-states soon set up a government modeled on Athens's democracy.

The people of a democratic city-state were not all considered equal. Strict rules determined which members of society were entitled to the rights of citizens. In Athens, for example, only free men over the age of twenty who had been born to Athenian parents could vote in the Assembly, the governing body that decided on public policies. At age thirty, Athenian citizens gained the right to serve as jurors and help make laws.

Beneath the privileged upper class in Greek society was a large group of foreign residents known as metics. Members of the metic class often worked as merchants, craftsmen, manufacturers, doctors, teachers, or in other skilled trades. While metics might earn great riches, they were usually forbidden to own land, and they had no political power.

The third and lowest class was made up of slaves. Even the poorest citizen or metic owned at least one slave, while rich households might own as many as fifty. Slaves had no political rights. Some masters allowed their slaves to live and work on their own, in return for a share of their wages. Slaves who earned enough money were sometimes able to purchase their freedom.

Greek wives and mothers were honored in their homes, and they played an active role in some religious celebrations. However, women of all classes were largely excluded from the public life of the city-states. They could not move about freely in public, buy or sell property, or participate in government.

Greek myths reflect the social conventions of the time. The women of mythology live in a restricted and male-dominated world. Women are portrayed in the home, where they are often seen spinning or weaving. However, there are many Greek myths that include powerful goddesses and resourceful heroines.

PART 1: Who Were the Greeks?

Gods on the Mountaintop

Apollo was said to have ridden across the sky every day in a golden chariot, representing the sun.

The ancient Greeks were **polytheists**, meaning they believed in multiple deities. In fact, they believed in countless gods, goddesses, and other divine beings. The gods controlled every aspect of nature and human life. They made the sun rise and set, the stars shine, the rains fall, and the crops grow. Gods were the reason that people fell in love, gave birth, and suffered from illness. Gods even looked after people in the afterlife. They lived forever and, with a few exceptions, had unlimited powers.

Apart from their extraordinary abilities, most gods and goddesses were very much like mortal men and women. They ate, drank, slept, played games, fell in love, and quarreled. They looked like humans, only much larger and more beautiful. They also took a great interest in human affairs. Gods and goddesses often disguised themselves as mortals and walked the earth, where they rewarded the good and punished the proud and wicked.

The twelve most important Greek deities lived in magnificent palaces at the top of Mount Olympus. The king of the Olympian gods was Zeus, ruler of the sky and earth. Zeus shared his power with his brother Poseidon, lord of the sea. He had three sisters: Hera, who was also his wife and queen of the immortals; Hestia, goddess of the hearth; and Demeter, goddess of agriculture. Also seated on the thrones of Olympus were seven of Zeus's children: Athena, Aphrodite, Apollo, Artemis, Ares, Hephaestus, and Hermes. Some sources include Hades, ruler of the underworld, in the list of Olympian gods. The family tree on page 25 shows the connections among the Olympians and their special areas of power and responsibility.

Occasionally it was said that mortals would venture up to Olympus, or gods would come down to greet them. Some of the greatest heroes were said to have been the children of Zeus. Hercules was one such demigod, and when he died, he was brought up to Olympus to sit at Zeus' side. However, it was very presumptuous for a mortal to attempt to sit beside gods. Bellerophon, another hero, decided that he was part god and tried to fly the winged horse Pegasus up to the top of Mount Olympus. Zeus, furious, made sure Bellerophon plummeted to his death. Read more about this on page 71.

A World of Worship

Athletic competitions, including discus, were part of religious festivals that celebrated the gods.

The gods and goddesses were an important part of daily life in Greece. Worship was conducted both individually at the home and at large festivals with the entire community. Worshippers offered regular prayers at altars they made in their houses. Greeks also prayed at shrines, sanctuaries, and temples scattered across the countryside. Religious places ranged from caves to crossroads to mountaintops.

At special times throughout the year, all the people of a city-state joined together to celebrate religious festivals. These elaborate ceremonies often began with a grand procession to the temple of the god or goddess who had been adopted as the **patron** deity, or special protector, of the polis. At the temple, worshippers honored the deity with prayers, music, dancing, and gifts of food, wine, and sacrificial animals.

A few festivals united all Greeks in worship. The highlight of these **Panhellenic** festivals was the athletic competitions. Thousands of people gathered to watch as athletes from every polis strived to honor and impress the gods with their skills in running, wrestling, discus throwing, chariot racing, and other sports. The most famous Panhellenic festival was held every four years at Olympia, a center for the worship of Zeus. This glorious celebration was the inspiration for our modern Olympic Games.

Myths were an essential part of every aspect of Greek life. In the home, parents used myths and entertaining stories to instruct their children. In the marketplace or the Assembly, men traded songs and stories based on mythological themes. They debated the will of the gods and based philosophical arguments on myth. At festivals and other gatherings, myths were recited as poetry. Sometimes playwrights rewrote the myths so they could be performed on stage. To the ancient Greeks, these myths were more than just good stories. They were the threads in the tapestry of Greek culture.

FAMILY TREE *of the* OLYMPIANS

The most important Greek deities were the twelve gods and goddesses known as the Olympians. Some sources include Hades in this list, even though his home was the underworld rather than Mount Olympus. Later lists sometimes add Dionysus, the popular Greek god of wine and merriment.

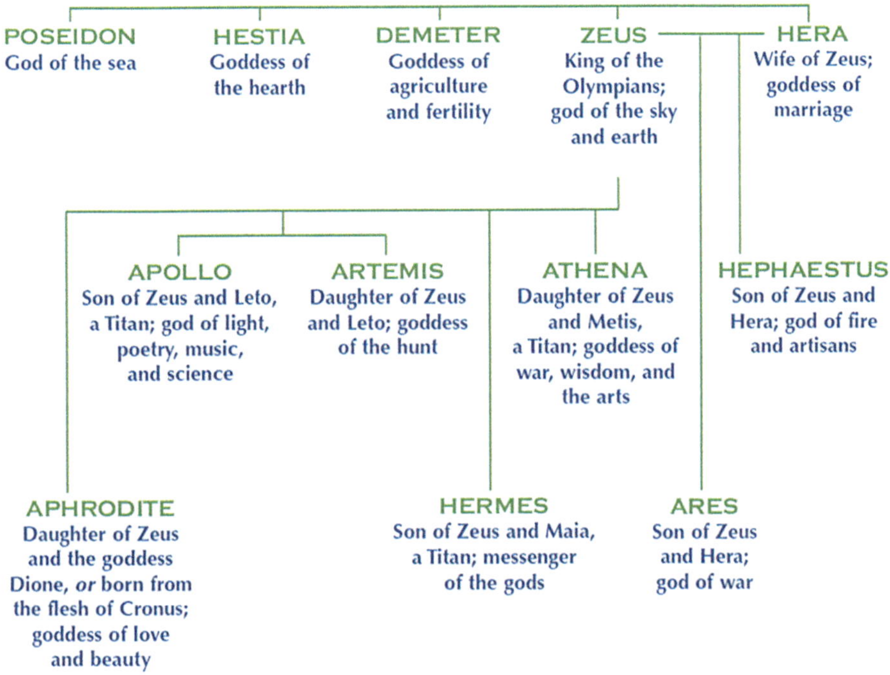

WORLD MYTHOLOGIES

MYTHS OF THE ANCIENT GREEKS

PART 2: Stories and Myths

The Beginning of All

This famous painting by Goya depicts Cronus eating his divine children.

The Greeks, like people throughout history, came up with their own origin stories to explain the creation of the world. Some stories were very specific and explained the origins of particular cities, social groups, and customs. Others dealt with the question "how did we come to be?" Many addressed the creation of the universe, and the beginnings of the gods.

Because myths were passed down orally, growing and changing with each retelling, there are often many different versions of the same story. This version of the Greek creation myth comes mainly from a long poem called *Theogony* ("**Genealogy** of the Gods"), written by the poet Hesiod around the eighth century BCE. Hesiod based his poem on a variety of traditional stories. He organized and connected these age-old tales to come up with a grand narrative that traced the development of the world all the way from an empty void to an orderly society controlled by the gods. *Theogony* described the struggle among three generations of gods and the triumph of the Olympians. It was one of the most popular and influential literary works of the Golden Age, inspiring countless poets, playwrights, historians, and philosophers.

Titans and Gods

In the beginning there was nothing but a vast shapeless void. out of the void emerged Mother Earth, along with Eros, the creative force that moves gods and men to desire. When Earth felt the touch of Eros, she grew lonely. So all by herself she produced a husband, who was named Father Sky.

Dramatis Personae

Dramatis Personae is a Latin phrase meaning "persons of the drama," or cast of characters. Here are the gods who play a role in the creation story of Greece:

Mother Earth First goddess of the earth; also known as Gaea (JEE-uh)

Eros One of the creative powers of the universe

Father Sky Ruler of the first generation of gods; also known as Uranus

Cyclopes (SIE-klah-peez) One-eyed giants

Hundred-Handers Monsters with fifty heads and one hundred arms

Titans Twelve immortal children of Earth and Sky

Cronus (KROW-nus) Ruler of the second generation of gods

Rhea (REE-uh) Wife of Cronus

Zeus (zoos) Ruler of the third generation of gods

Sky was a perfect fit for Earth, covering her on all sides with his great starry blanket. Out of their union came many remarkable children. There were three Cyclopes, gigantic creatures with a single eye in the middle of their foreheads. There were three Hundred-Handers, horrid monsters with fifty heads and a hundred arms sprouting from their shoulders. But the boldest of all were the twelve immortal giants called Titans.

Mother Earth loved all her children, no matter how big and ugly. But Father Sky looked upon his monstrous offspring with fear and horror. He bound the Cyclopes in chains and cast them down into **Tartarus**, the deepest part of the underworld. He sent the monstrous Hundred-Handers to the same gloomy region. For the bold Titans, he dreamed up an even crueler fate. As these immortal children were born, Sky stuffed them back inside Earth, where they twisted and turned, tormenting their mother.

At last Earth could take no more of Sky's heartless behavior. She begged her children to help her take revenge on her husband. At the thought of confronting their mighty father, all the children were seized with a paralyzing fear—all, that is, but the youngest Titan, Cronus.

Mother Earth was delighted with her son's brave spirit. She made a long, jagged sickle and gave it to Cronus. She hid him in a dark corner of her bedchamber. Soon Sky came once again to cover Earth with his starry blanket. This time Cronus was ready. With a slash of the saw-toothed blade, the young Titan sliced off his father's private parts and tossed them into the sea, stripping the god of his limitless power.

After Cronus conquered Sky, he sent the wounded god into exile. Then he took his father's place as ruler of the world. Cronus freed his fellow Titans from bondage and married his fair-haired sister Rhea. In time Rhea bore six splendid children: Hestia, Demeter, Hera, Hades, Poseidon, and Zeus. But, like his father before him, Cronus loathed his children. Through a dreadful

The Titan Rhea birthed the first six gods.

prophecy, he had learned that he was destined to lose his throne to his son Zeus, just as he himself had overthrown Father Sky. So the king of the gods kept a sharp watch, and as each one of his immortal children was born, he swallowed it whole.

Rhea grieved long and hard for her lost children. Finally, as the birth of her sixth child drew near, she begged her parents for help. Mother Earth and Father Sky were moved by their daughter's sad story. Together, they contrived a scheme to conceal their grandchild's birth. Under the cover of darkness, they sent Rhea to the island of Crete. There, Zeus was born in a deep, dark, mountain cave. Leaving the infant in the care of the mountain **nymphs**, Rhea rushed home to her husband. She wrapped a huge stone in baby clothes and gave it to Cronus. The poor fool believed that the bundle was his newborn son. Grabbing the stone, he quickly gulped it down into his belly.

The seasons passed, and young Zeus grew in size, strength, and wisdom. It wasn't long before he was ready to face his cruel father. Once again, Mother Earth came to her grandson's aid. Using honeyed words, the cunning goddess persuaded Cronus to retain the handsome youth from Crete as his personal servant. She helped Zeus prepare a mixture of salt and mustard. The young god stirred the potion into a cup of sweet **nectar** and gave it to his father. Cronus drained the cup in a single gulp.

How Aphrodite Was Born

In Hesiod's version of the Greek creation story, the wounding of Father Sky leads to the birth of Aphrodite, goddess of love and beauty. Here the poet describes what happened after Cronus threw Sky's private parts into the sea.

> White foam issued from the divine flesh, and in the foam a girl began to grow ... She stepped out, a goddess, tender and beautiful, and round her slender feet the green grass shot up. She is called Aphrodite ["foam-born"] by gods and men, because she grew in the froth ... Eros [Desire] and beautiful Passion were her attendants both at her birth and at her first going to join the family of the gods. The rights and privileges assigned to her from the beginning and recognized by men and gods are these: to preside over the whispers and smiles and tricks which girls employ, and the sweet delight and tenderness of love.

His belly began to roll and rumble. Suddenly the great god vomited up the stone he had swallowed years before. Then, one by one, Cronus threw up his children.

Rejoicing in their freedom, the immortal children of Cronus went to live on towering Mount Olympus. Soon a terrible war raged in the heavens. On one side were the gods of Olympus, with Zeus as their leader. On the other side were Cronus and the Titans, who swore that they would never yield power to the young rivals. For ten long years, the enemies fought without ceasing. Finally, Zeus traveled down to Tartarus, the dark underworld where Father Sky had imprisoned the Cyclopes and the Hundred-Handers.

The Dance of Curetes was used to distract Cronus while the infant Zeus was hidden away. The clashing sounds of the sword and the shield prevented Zeus's cries from reaching Cronus.

He freed the monsters from their gloomy dungeons, earning their undying loyalty. The grateful Cyclopes forged thunder and the lightning bolt and gave these to Zeus to make him master of gods and men. The Hundred-Handers, dreadful and strong, pledged to join the Olympians in their fierce struggle with the Titans.

That very day a grim battle began, involving all the gods and monsters. The earth quaked and the mountains trembled as the two sides collided. Loud battle cries rose to the heavens, and the sound of pounding feet sank all the way to Tartarus. At the very front of the battle lines, the Hundred-Handers hurled huge boulders, which rained down on the Titans in a deadly shower. Then Zeus revealed his full power. Charging through the skies, the great god cast lightning and thunder, blinding his enemies and enclosing them in a whirlwind of fire.

At that, the battle turned, and the mighty Titans were overpowered. Binding their fallen enemies in chains, the Hundred-Handers carried them far below the ground to Tartarus. There the Titans dwell to this day, in a region so dark and dismal that even the gods grow pale when they hear its name mentioned.

> Mount Olympus trembled from base to summit as the immortal beings clashed.
>
> ~ Hesiod, eighth century BCE

Finally, the gods were free, and the Titans were imprisoned. Each powerful god and goddess had their own powers and controlled different parts of the world. Demeter became the goddess of harvest and crops, Hestia became the goddess of hearth and home, and Hera became the goddess of childbirth and marriage. The gods drew lots to divide up parts of the world. Poseidon won dominion over the sea. Hades drew the vast underworld as his kingdom. Zeus became ruler of the heavens and the surface of the earth, head of all the gods and immortals.

The Stories of Prometheus and Pandora

Prometheus was a Titan, but he was also a trickster and the creator and champion of humans.

The Greeks had many different stories about how humans came to be. In some of the earliest tales, humanity sprouted from the earth. In others, the gods made people from divine materials or dirt. However, the most famous story is the myth of Prometheus and the humans.

Prometheus, whose name means "forethought," was a Titan. In the great battle of the gods, he foresaw the fall of the Titans and decided to fight on the side of the Olympians instead. As a reward, Zeus spared Prometheus and his brother Epimetheus, or "afterthought," when the defeated Titans were imprisoned in the underworld. The brothers were even entrusted with an important task: the creation of all mortal creatures, including man.

Prometheus was not only the creator of mankind but also its greatest champion. In his best-known myth, the Titan defied Zeus to bring men the gift of fire, one of the essentials of civilization. This act of rebellion against authority made Prometheus a favorite subject for artists, philosophers, poets, and playwrights. One of the most famous retellings of his story was the play *Prometheus Bound*, traditionally said to have been written by the Greek playwright Aeschylus in the fifth century BCE. This dramatic masterpiece showed the noble Titan bravely enduring a horrible punishment for putting the good of mortal men above the will of the gods.

Closely connected with the Prometheus story was the myth of Pandora's box. According to this ancient tale, the first woman was created by the gods to punish man for accepting the gift of fire. Before Pandora was created, the world was a paradise. With her arrival on earth came all the evils that have plagued humankind ever since. The story of Pandora not only explained the troubles of the world but also justified the dominance of men over women in ancient Greece.

Dramatis Personae

Zeus (zoos) King of the Olympians

Prometheus (pro-MEE-thee-us) Titan who was the champion of mankind

Epimetheus (ep-ih-MEE-thee-us) Foolish brother of Prometheus

Hephaestus (huh-FESS-tus) God of fire and artisans

Pandora (pan-DOR-a) First woman

Prometheus, Champion of Men

There was once a time when there were no mortal creatures, only gods. From his golden throne on Mount Olympus, Zeus commanded Prometheus and his brother Epimetheus to fill up the vast empty world. Together, the two Titans created a host of creatures to populate the land, sea, and air. Then Prometheus took clay, kneaded it with water, and made man. This last creation was also his finest, because it was formed in the image of the gods. Unlike all the other creatures, man walked upright, gazing not down at the earth but up to the starry heavens.

After the task of creation was completed, Epimetheus persuaded Prometheus to let him deal out all the gifts mortal creatures would need to survive. To some animals, he gave sharp claws and teeth. To others went fur for warmth or a thick hide for armor. The busy Titan gave out size, strength, speed, and all the other faculties for preservation. But Epimetheus, who was not so wise as he might be, forgot to leave something for man.

When Prometheus came to examine the distribution, he was sorely troubled. How could he protect his favorite creation? Only one gift remained, one surpassing all the others. This was the gift of fire. But Zeus had decreed that men should never have fire, because that would make them too much like the gods. For an instant Prometheus hesitated. Then, moved by his great love for mankind, the Titan chose to defy the almighty god.

Stealthily, Prometheus crept to the top of Mount Olympus. He sneaked into the fiery forge of Hephaestus, the blacksmith god. The Titan stole a glowing ember from the furnace and hid it inside the hollow stem of a plant. Then Prometheus returned to earth with the fire of the immortals. This divine gift raised man far above the other animals. With fire he could make tools to work the earth, weapons to subdue his enemies, and goods for art

Prometheus endures his punishment for stealing fire. An eagle is picking out his liver.

and trade. Along with his great gift, Prometheus also taught men how to build dwellings, sail the seas, use letters and numbers, and many other skills to enrich and empower them.

Before long, Zeus looked down at the earth and saw the radiant light of fire. Instantly the wise god knew that Prometheus had defied his command. With an angry rumble of thunder, he ordered Hephaestus to carry the rebellious Titan to a remote mountaintop and chain him to the rocks. Then Zeus sent a monstrous eagle to torment Prometheus. Every morning the eagle spread its long wings and flew to the mountain. The whole day through, it fed on the helpless prisoner's liver. Every night, the liver grew back, and the next day the torture began again.

Prometheus endured this terrible punishment a long, long time; some say thirty years, some say thirty thousand. At long last a great hero named Heracles killed the giant eagle, and Zeus relented, freeing the Titan. The god decreed that Prometheus must forever wear a ring made from his broken chains as a sign of his imprisonment. That is why, to this day, men wear rings, in honor of their greatest champion.

A Dangerous Box

After Zeus imprisoned Prometheus for giving humans the gift of fire, he turned his attention to the men who had accepted the Titan's gift. For these, too, the angry god devised a dreadful punishment. He ordered Hephaestus to make the first woman. The blacksmith god created woman in the image of the immortal goddesses. Each

Sacrificing the Bones

One variation of the Prometheus myth explained the origins of the Greek practice of animal sacrifice. According to this story, Zeus demanded that men sacrifice an ox to show their obedience to the gods. The men asked Prometheus which portion of the animal must go to the gods and which parts they could keep. As this passage from Hesiod's *Theogony* explains, the Titan tricked Zeus into accepting the bones of the beast. From then on, when the Greeks sacrificed an animal, they burned the bones and feasted on the choicest meat.

> Prometheus cheerfully butchered a great ox and served it up, trying to befuddle Zeus' wits. For Zeus he set out flesh [meat] ... laid out on the oxhide and covered with its paunch [to look unappetizing]. But for the others he set out the animal's white bones artfully dressed out and covered with [slabs of] shining fat. And then the Father of gods and men said to him, "... My celebrated lord, how unevenly you have divided the portions." ... And Prometheus, whose mind was devious, smiled softly and remembered his trickery: "Zeus most glorious, greatest of the everlasting gods, choose whichever of these your heart desires." ... With both his hands he [Zeus] took up the gleaming fat. Anger seethed in his lungs and bile rose to his heart when he saw the ox's white bones [hidden under the fat].

Pandora was the first woman and is said to be responsible for releasing sorrows into the world.

of the Olympians gave her a gift. Golden Aphrodite endowed her with grace and beauty. Athena dressed her in a shimmering gown and placed a wreath of luscious flowers on her head. From the other gods came talent for playing music, skill in weaving and embroidery, and other charms to make her irresistible to men. Finally, Hermes filled the heart of the lovely maiden with cunning lies and deceit. Zeus named this beautiful curse Pandora, which means "all-gifted." Then he sent her to Epimetheus as a gift.

Now, farsighted Prometheus had told his scatterbrained brother to beware of gifts from Zeus. One look at the enchanting maiden, however, and the foolish Titan forgot his brother's warning. Epimetheus welcomed Pandora with open arms. He took her into his home and made her his wife. And with woman came all the evils that have plagued humankind ever since.

> Pandora took the lid off the big jar with her hands and scattered all the miseries that spell sorrow for men.
>
> ~ Hesiod, eighth century BCE

For Pandora had brought with her a large storage jar (or, some say, a wooden box), given to her as a bridal gift by Zeus. The wily god had sealed the container and told her never to open it. For a time, Pandora heeded his command. But one day, when her husband was away from the house, her curiosity got the better of her. Pandora tiptoed into the room where Epimetheus had placed the jar. She reached up with both hands and pried off the lid. Suddenly out flew ten thousand horrors: Pain, Sorrow, Envy, Spite, Madness, Disease, War, Death, and many other evils.

Pandora slammed down the lid, but to no avail. The horrors had flown out into the world. Only one thing saved humanity from total destruction. Clinging to the rim of the jar was Hope. Hope became humanity's saving grace. To this day Hope never entirely leaves us, and with its help we are able to endure all misfortunes brought on by the world.

PART 2: Stories and Myths

The Seasons and Persephone

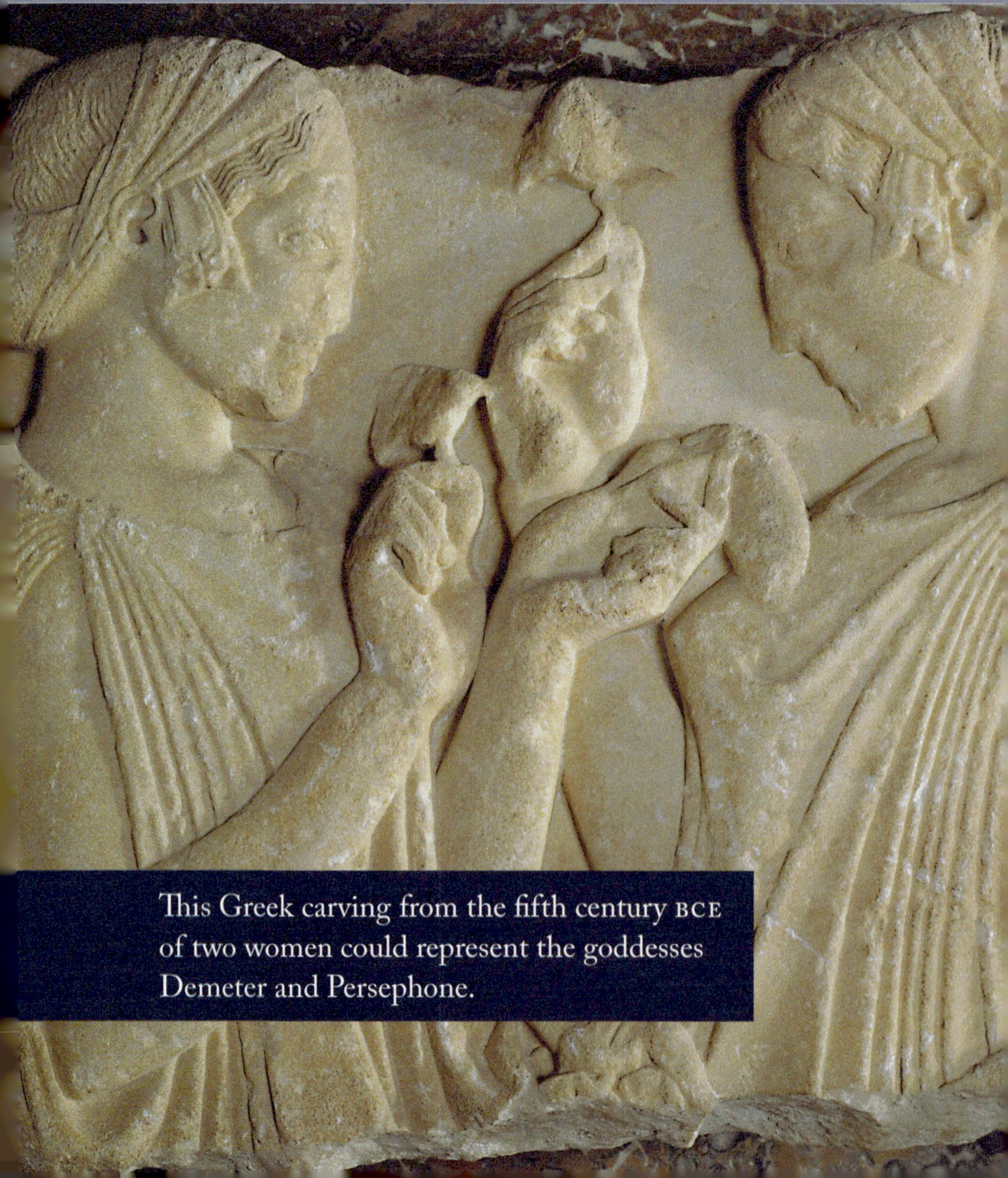

This Greek carving from the fifth century BCE of two women could represent the goddesses Demeter and Persephone.

In Greece, one of the most revered and important goddesses was Demeter, goddess of agriculture. Demeter caused the crops to grow and the harvest to come. Demeter had a daughter she loved very much. According to mythology, her daughter Persephone was kidnapped by Hades, god of the underworld. Demeter became furious and refused to let the crops grow. Finally, Zeus intervened and worked out an agreement. Persephone was to live with her mother every spring and summer, only to return to the underworld for the winter. This story of Persephone and Demeter explained the changing seasons.

The Greeks honored Demeter and Persephone with a festival known as the Greater Eleusinian Mysteries, held each fall in the city of Eleusis, west of Athens. People came from all over the Greek world to join in this important celebration. Because the participants were required to take a vow of secrecy, we have only a general idea of what happened during the Mysteries. We know that the festival began with a torch-lit procession from Athens to the temple of Demeter in Eleusis. There, worshippers may have presented offerings of honey, fruit, grain, and poppies, which were a symbol of sleep and death. The story of Persephone's abduction and Demeter's search may have been recited or performed. The festival probably ended with the triumphant return of Persephone, perhaps represented by ripened grain. The joyous rites of the Eleusinian Mysteries celebrated not only the cycles of nature but also the immortality of the soul and the promise of happiness in the afterlife.

Dramatis Personae

Demeter (dih-MEE-ter) Goddess of agriculture and fertility

Persephone (per-SEH-fuh-nee) Daughter of Demeter and Zeus; wife of Hades

Hades (HAY-deez) God of the underworld

Zeus (zoos) King of the Olympians

Celeus (SEE-lee-us) Mortal king of Eleusis

Metaneira (may-tuh-NEE-ruh) Queen of Eleusis

Demophoon (dee-moh-FOH-on) Son of Celeus and Metaneira

Hermes (HER-meez) Messenger of the gods

The Kidnapping of Persephone

In the early ages of humanity, the earth always bloomed. From her throne atop Mount Olympus, golden-haired Demeter sprinkled the seeds on the ground. The goddess tended the fruit trees and ripened the grain in the fields. By her side as she worked was her young daughter Persephone, as sweet and delicate as a springtime flower.

One day Hades, lord of the underworld, looked up from his dark kingdom. He saw the beautiful young maiden and fell in love. Hades went to his brother Zeus, who was the girl's father, and asked for Persephone's hand in marriage. Now, Zeus did not wish to oppose his brother, but he knew that Demeter would never consent to the match. So the king of the gods promised to come up with a plan to help Hades steal Persephone from her mother.

A day came when Persephone was apart from her mother, playing with her friends in a green meadow. Seeing the girl unattended, Zeus asked Mother Earth to cover the meadow with flowers. Soon sweet-smelling roses and colorful lilies mingled with bright crocuses and tiny violets. Persephone wandered farther and farther away from her companions, filling her apron with blossoms. At the edge of the meadow, she saw the prettiest flower of all, a silvery iris with a heavenly fragrance. Bending down, the girl reached for the tempting blossom. Suddenly the earth gaped open, and out thundered Hades in his golden chariot. Persephone cried out in terror as the dark lord grabbed her. She struggled but could not escape him. With a flick of his

Hades arrived in his dark chariot, taking Persephone down to the underworld to be his bride.

The Afterlife of the Greeks

In ancient times most Greeks believed that after death, a person's spirit went to the kingdom of Hades. This vast underworld realm was divided into three regions. Most spirits wandered for eternity in a bare, colorless meadow where there was neither pleasure nor pain. The souls of those who had been especially virtuous or heroic in life went to a heavenly paradise called the Elysian Fields or Islands of the Blessed. The souls of the wicked were cast into the deepest, darkest part of the underworld, Tartarus. The Greek philosopher Plato described the division of the souls in this passage from one of his dialogues (works written in the form of a conversation).

> Listen, then, as story-tellers say, to a very pretty tale, which I dare say that you may be disposed to regard as a fable only, but which, as I believe, is a true tale ... Now in the days of Cronos there existed a law respecting the destiny of man, which has always been, and still continues to be in Heaven,—that he who has lived all his life in justice and holiness shall go, when he is dead, to the Islands of the Blessed, and dwell there in perfect happiness out of the reach of evil; but that he who has lived unjustly and impiously shall go to the house of vengeance and punishment, which is called Tartarus ... They who have been guilty of the worst crimes ... [endure] for ever the most terrible and painful and fearful sufferings as the penalty of their sins.

whip, Hades turned his horses and carried the weeping maiden down into the misty realms of darkness.

From afar, Demeter heard her daughter's piercing cries. Speeding over land and sea, she came to the meadow, but there was no trace of Persephone. The goddess threw a black cloak over her shoulders and went in search of her missing child. For nine days and nights, she wandered the earth, a blazing torch held high in her hands. All this time, the grieving goddess did not eat or drink or bathe her skin in water. At length, Demeter came to Helios, god of the sun, who sees all things in his daily passage across the heavens. And Helios told her that Zeus himself had given Persephone to be the bride of Hades.

> Hades seized [Persephone] and took her loudly crying in his chariot down to his realm of mist and gloom.
>
> ~ *Homeric Hymn to Demeter*

When she heard these words, Demeter was filled with an even more terrible grief and a great savage anger. Leaving her throne, she went to dwell among mortals. Disguised as an old woman, the goddess roamed across farm fields and cities. At last she came to the land of Eleusis, which was ruled by the wise king Celeus. There, Demeter rested in the shade of an olive tree, beside a well where women drew water. In time the four daughters of the king came to fill their shining vessels. They saw an old woman in a dark cloak, her head bent with sorrow. Taking pity, the girls spoke kindly to Demeter and invited her home to the palace.

Eagerly, the good maidens led Demeter to their mother, Queen Metaneira. When the disguised goddess entered the queen's chamber, the whole room filled with a heavenly radiance. Metaneira turned pale with fear and wonder. Rising, she offered her bright throne to the mysterious guest. Demeter insisted on taking a low stool instead. The queen filled a cup with sweet red wine. The unhappy goddess would drink only coarse barley water. Impressed by Demeter's grace and dignity, Metaneira suspected that her guest was a noblewoman fallen on ill fortune. So the queen asked Demeter to join the royal household as nursemaid to her newborn son, Demophoon.

After the kidnapping of Persephone, Demeter was inconsolable. She left the world to waste while she grieved.

For many days Demeter lived in the palace and found some comfort holding the little prince in her arms. Indeed, she became so fond of Demophoon that she decided to make him immortal. Each day, the goddess rubbed the baby with **ambrosia**, the food of the gods. Each night, while the family slept, she placed him in the hearth fire to burn off his mortal parts. The boy soon grew as strong and healthy as a young god. But alas, the queen grew suspicious of the mysterious nursemaid. One night she went spying, and when she crept into the kitchen, she saw Demeter roasting Demophoon in the flames. The queen shrieked in alarm, and the ritual was ruined. Snatching the baby from the fire, Demeter angrily cursed the foolishness of mortals. Shedding her disguise, she revealed herself in all her bright and terrible beauty. The glorious goddess demanded that the people of Eleusis build her a splendid temple, where she could teach them to perform her secret rites and win back her favor. Then, with a flash of divine light, she stormed out of the palace.

The people were quick to obey Demeter's commands. As soon as they completed the temple, the goddess sat down inside it. And there she stayed, still yearning for her lost daughter.

Now came a cruel year for humankind. Demeter would not make the seeds sprout in the ground, and the green earth turned brown and barren. Zeus looked down from Mount Olympus and saw that the entire race of humans was threatened with starvation. He sent a messenger to Demeter, asking her to restore the earth's fruitfulness, but the angry goddess refused him. After that, all the gods and goddesses came, one by one,

Demeter's Temple

The best-known version of the myth of Demeter and Persephone comes from the *Homeric Hymn to Demeter*. This long poem was part of a collection of sacred poetry popular during the Golden Age. The ancient Greeks believed that the Homeric Hymns were the work of Homer, the revered author of the *Iliad* and the *Odyssey*. Today, scholars think that the poems were actually written by later poets working in the same style and tradition as Homer. In this passage from the *Homeric Hymn to Demeter*, the goddess orders the people of Eleusis to build the temple that will become her center of worship.

> [Demeter] was terribly angry in her heart. Forthwith she said to well-girded [dressed] Metaneira: "... Let all the people build me a great temple and an altar below it. ... And I myself will teach my rites, that hereafter you may reverently perform them and so win the favor of my heart."
>
> ... So Celeus called the countless people to an assembly and bade them make a goodly temple for rich-haired Demeter and an altar upon the rising hillock. And they obeyed him right speedily and harkened to his voice, doing as he commanded ...
>
> Now when they had finished building and had drawn back from their toil, they went every man to his house. But golden-haired Demeter sat there apart from all the blessed gods and stayed, wasting with yearning for her ... daughter.

Persephone would have been returned to her mother full time, but she tasted the fruit of the pomegranate.

begging Demeter to return to Olympus. Still she refused, declaring that the world would never know another harvest until her eyes once again beheld her daughter. Finally, Zeus relented. Sending Hermes as his messenger to the dark underworld, he ordered Hades to release Persephone.

The king of the dead smiled grimly when he heard his brother's command. Without a word, he harnessed the horses to his golden chariot and handed the reins to Hermes. Then Hades called for Persephone. All this time, the shy young bride had sat without eating or sleeping, pining for her mother. Now she sprang up rejoicing. As she mounted the chariot, Hades asked her to think kindly of the husband who so dearly loved her. With a gentle sigh and a sly glance over his shoulder, he gave Persephone a juicy, red **pomegranate** for her journey. For the cunning god knew that those who taste the food of the dead can never return to the land of the living.

The black steeds charged from the palace of Hades. Swiftly, the chariot flew through the air to Demeter's temple in Eleusis. When the goddess saw her dear child, she rushed forth and embraced her. But as she held Persephone in her arms, her heart was seized with a sudden misgiving. Fearfully, Demeter asked her daughter if she had tasted any food in Hades' dark kingdom. And the girl, in her innocence, assured her mother that she had eaten only one seed of a pomegranate.

Demeter's heart sank. Then, in his wisdom, Zeus issued a new command that would satisfy both mother and husband. Persephone would spend one-third of each year in the kingdom of the dead with Hades and the other two-thirds in the world of light with her mother.

Consoled by this ruling, Demeter flew over the barren earth, causing the flowers to bloom and the fields to swell with grain. Next she went to Celeus, king of Eleusis, and taught him her sacred rites. Then the goddess returned to Mount Olympus, where she and Persephone rejoiced in the company of the immortals.

Spring returns every year with the return of Demeter to the world. She spends her time with her mother, and their joy brings life to the crops and flowers. Yet, in winter Persephone dwells in the house of Hades, and Demeter puts on her dark cloak, and the earth is barren. And so it is that Demeter brings us the seasons.

The Hero Theseus and the Minotaur

The Minotaur is one of the most famous monsters of Greek mythology.

The adventures of heroes were popular and enduring stories in ancient Greece, and over time they became myths. Many of these heroes had incredible powers. These mortal men used their fantastic strengths and talents to perform amazing tasks. Although they had superhuman abilities, such heroes often had very human faults. The emotions, conflicts, and challenges heroes faced were often those ordinary people dealt with every day, only on a much grander scale.

Many of the heroes in Greek mythology had at least one immortal parent. The gods played an active role in their lives, either aiding or opposing their quests. While there were a few Greek heroines, most heroic mortals were men. However, women often inspired a hero's adventures or helped him perform his great deeds.

The hero Theseus was sometimes said to have two fathers: Poseidon, god of the sea, and Aegeus, a mortal king. Theseus's most famous adventure took place on the island of Crete, in the days of Minos, the mythical founder of the Minoan civilization. Minos was a powerful king with a nasty problem. His wife had given birth to a hideous man-eating monster known as the Minotaur. The king confined the Minotaur in the labyrinth, a vast maze beneath his palace. Every nine years he forced the people of Athens to send a **tribute** of young men and women to feed to the beast. Theseus ended the tribute and proved his heroic strength and courage by killing the Minotaur.

The story of Theseus's triumph over Minos offered a mythological explanation for the fall of the Minoans and the rise of the civilizations of mainland Greece. To the people of ancient Athens, the myth also explained the founding of their city-state and its democratic form of government. Our version of this popular tale comes largely from a collection of biographies known as *Plutarch's Lives*, composed by the Greek writer and moralist Plutarch around 75 CE.

Dramatis Personae

Aegeus (EE-jee-us) King of Athens; mortal father of Theseus

Pittheus (PIT-thoos) Grandfather of Theseus

Aethra (EE-thruh) Mother of Theseus

Theseus (THEE-see-us) Athenian hero

Poseidon (puh-SIE-dun) God of the sea; immortal father of Theseus

Medea (muh-DEE-uh) Sorceress and wife of Aegeus

Minos (MIE-nus) King of Crete

Aphrodite (af-ruh-DIE-tee) Goddess of love and beauty

Ariadne (ar-ee-ADD-nee) Daughter of King Minos

Daedalus (DED-uh-lus) Master craftsman and inventor

Dionysus (die-uh-NIE-sus) God of wine

Theseus Conquers the Labyrinth

King Aegeus of Athens was weighed down with troubles. He had been married twice, but he still had no son to inherit his throne. So Aegeus went to visit his wise friend Pittheus, the governor of a southern city. And Pittheus gave the king his only daughter, fair Aethra, to love.

When the time came for Aegeus to return to Athens, he led Aethra to a huge boulder. The king placed his sword and sandals in a hollow beneath the rock. Then he gave Aethra a command. If she gave birth to a son who grew up worthy and strong, she must bring him to this spot. If the boy could lift the boulder and retrieve the hidden tokens, she should send him to Athens. All this must be done in great secrecy. For Aegeus had many enemies who would gladly murder the king's heir to secure the throne for themselves.

In the course of time, Aethra had a son and named him Theseus. Remembering Aegeus's warning, she concealed the boy's identity by claiming that his father was Poseidon, god of the sea. To this day there are some who say that her story was true. Some even say that Aethra was loved by both Aegeus and Poseidon, so that Theseus had two fathers, one mortal and one divine. Whatever his true parentage, the boy grew up strong and bold. When he reached manhood, his mother took him to the boulder. Theseus lifted the heavy rock with ease and found the hidden sword and sandals. Then Aethra revealed the strange story of his birth and told her son to take the tokens to Athens.

There were two routes to Athens: the easy journey by sea and the more dangerous passage along roads infested with robbers and murderers. Theseus's mother and grandfather begged him to take the safer path, but the young man longed to prove his strength and courage through noble acts. So Theseus set out by land, and on his long journey he fought and killed many evil men and wild beasts.

The Strength of Hercules

For the heroes of Greek mythology, the most important goal in life was glory. Nearly every action taken by a heroic mortal was inspired by the desire to earn glory through brave and noble deeds. Plutarch tells us that Theseus took the hazardous route to Athens out of admiration for Heracles, the most glorious of all Greek heroes. In his story Plutarch refers to Heracles by his Roman name, Hercules.

> [Theseus], it seems, had long since been secretly fired by the glory of Hercules, held him in the highest estimation, and was never more satisfied than in listening to any that gave an account of him ... In the night his dreams were all of that hero's actions and in the day a continual emulation [jealous ambition] stirred him up to perform the like. Besides, they were related, being born of cousins ... He thought it therefore a dishonorable thing, and not to be endured, that Hercules should go out everywhere, and purge both land and sea from wicked men, and he himself should fly from the like adventures that actually came in his way; ... not showing ... the greatness of his birth by noble and worthy actions ...
>
> With this mind and these thoughts, he set forward with a decision to do injury to nobody, but to repel and revenge himself on all those that should offer any.

At last Theseus reached Athens, where news of his heroic exploits had already made him famous. But the end of his journey only brought new dangers, for King Aegeus had grown old and fearful, and in his folly, he had married the sorceress Medea. Through her evil arts, the witch knew instantly that Theseus was her husband's son. In her jealousy and spite, she decided to kill him.

Medea persuaded Aegeus that the mysterious young stranger was a dangerous assassin. Advising her husband to invite Theseus to a feast, she prepared a cup of poisoned wine. When the guests arrived, Aegeus offered Theseus the deadly cup. Then the king's eyes fell to the stranger's sandals and the sword at his side. Recognizing the tokens, Aegeus knocked the cup from Theseus's hand. With great joy he embraced his long-lost son. The king banished Medea from the land. Gathering together all the citizens of Athens, he proclaimed Theseus his heir, and the people received the young hero gladly.

After Theseus joined his father, he learned that a terrible burden hung over Athens. Many years earlier, a son of King Minos of Crete had been killed on a visit to the city. To avenge his son's death, Minos had sent his powerful navy to harass Athens. He had also prayed to his father, almighty Zeus, who sent a plague of diseases, drought, and famine. In order to end their misery, the Athenians agreed to send Crete a tribute of seven young men and seven maidens every nine years. The victims were cast into the labyrinth beneath Minos's palace at Knossos. In that twisting, turning maze dwelt the Minotaur, a fierce flesh-eating monster with a human body and the head of a bull. The doomed youths wandered in the labyrinth, with no hope of escape, until one by one they were captured and devoured.

Soon the time came to draw lots for the next tribute. Theseus volunteered to take the place of one of the young Athenians. Aegeus could not bear to lose his newfound son. He begged Theseus to reconsider, but the prince was determined to kill the Minotaur and end the dreadful sacrifices. So the king outfitted the tribute ship with two sails, one black and one white. If Theseus died in Crete, the ship's pilot would raise the black sail on the return voyage. If the prince triumphed over the Minotaur, he would hoist the white sail with his own hands, so that his anxious father could see the sign and know he was safe.

> [Medea] was aware of Theseus, and … she easily persuaded Aegeus to kill him with poison at a banquet.
>
> ~ Plutarch, first–second centuries CE

Like all sensible travelers, Theseus began his journey with offerings to the immortals. Aphrodite, goddess of love, was especially pleased with the handsome young hero. The goddess watched over his voyage, and when the Athenians reached Crete, she touched the heart of Minos's daughter Ariadne. The fair princess had come to the seaside with her father to watch the arrival of the tribute ship. The instant she saw Theseus step ashore, she fell deeply in love.

That night Ariadne came to the prison where the Athenians lay awaiting their sacrifice. She pledged her love and promised to help Theseus survive the labyrinth. Ariadne handed the hero a ball of thread, given to her by Daedalus, the master craftsman who had built the labyrinth. Then she confided the builder's secret for escaping the baffling maze.

> Theseus, being driven by a storm upon the isle of Cyprus, … set [Ariadne] on shore, and left her there alone.
>
> ~ Plutarch, first–second centuries CE

The next morning, when the prisoners were cast into the labyrinth, Theseus tied one end of the string to the entrance. Slowly, he made his way through the dark, winding corridors, stepping over the bones of past victims. He heard the rumble of deep, raspy breathing. He felt a wave of heat and smelled the odor of death and decay. Rounding a bend, he saw the powerful manlike body and hideous bullhead of the Minotaur. With a roar, the beast attacked. The brave hero fought back with his sword. Long and grim was their battle. At last, with one mighty sweep of his blade, Theseus beheaded the monster.

Rewinding the thread, Theseus traced his way back through the labyrinth. Near the entrance, he found the other Athenians waiting. Together they fled to the harbor, where they knocked holes in the bottoms of Minos's ships so that the king could not pursue them. Then Theseus and the Athenians sailed for home, carrying Ariadne with them.

How the Minotaur Came to Be

Archaeologists investigating the ruins of the ancient palace at Knossos on Crete have found many images of the bull, a sacred animal to the people of the Minoan civilization. It is possible that Minoan priests wore masks that looked like bull heads during religious rituals, a practice that may have inspired the tale of the Minotaur. Mythology offered a more fantastic explanation for the monster, as described in this passage by the first-century BCE Greek historian Diodorus Siculus.

> It had been the custom of Minos annually to dedicate to Poseidon the fairest bull born in his herds and to sacrifice it to the god; but at the time in question there was born a bull of extraordinary beauty, and he sacrificed another from among those which were inferior, whereupon Poseidon becoming angry at Minos, caused his wife Pasiphae to [give] birth to the Minotaur, famed in the myth. This creature, they say, was of double form, the upper parts of the body as far as the shoulders being those of a bull and the remaining parts those of a man.

But Ariadne was not destined to reach Athens. When the ship stopped at an island to take on provisions, the princess fell asleep on the beach, and Theseus abandoned her. No one knows why the hero committed this heartless act. Some say that his ship was driven out to sea by a violent storm. Others claim that he left Ariadne willingly, because he loved another. Still others tell us that Dionysus, god of wine, appeared to Theseus in a dream and demanded the princess. According to this account, Dionysus and Ariadne married and lived together happily for many years. When his mortal wife died, the god placed her golden wedding crown among the stars, where it still twinkles in the night sky.

Theseus sailed on to Athens, where his father anxiously awaited him. So excited was the young hero over the successful completion of his journey that he forgot his promise to raise the white sail. Watching from a high cliff, Aegeus saw the dreaded black sail on the horizon. In his grief, the king threw himself off the rocks and perished in the sea that now bears the name Aegean.

As terrible as this tragedy was, Theseus then became king of Athens. Once he became king, Theseus expanded Athens into surrounding territories. Then he divided society into classes and established a democracy in which citizens had a share in their government. Theseus was credited with the advent of democracy. With Theseus's changes, Athens became the most powerful and prosperous city-state in all of Greece. Athens has honored Theseus to this day as their greatest hero.

PART 2: Stories and Myths

The Tragedy of Daedalus and Icarus

Daedalus and Icarus, as painted by Anthony van Dyck

An important theme in Greek mythology was **hubris**, or excessive pride. Many kings and heroes had achieved great things, owned great lands, or had great powers. Yet, as mortals, they were never as great as the gods. In the world of Greek mythology, the worst offense a mortal could commit was to claim they were equal to the gods. This was seen as a challenge by the Greek gods. Men and women might show their hubris by competing with the gods, disobeying their commands, or approaching them without an invitation.

Sometimes, mortals committed these acts unintentionally. For example, one myth told of a boy named Tiresias, who accidentally caught a glimpse of the goddess Athena while she was bathing in a mountain pool. Tiresias was struck blind for his offense. In other myths people guilty of hubris were skinned alive, wiped out by a thunderbolt, or turned into a rock or a spider.

One of the best-known stories about the perils of hubris is the story of Daedalus and Icarus. Daedalus was the master craftsman who designed the labyrinth, the setting for the tale of Theseus and the Minotaur. After Daedalus aided Theseus by revealing the secrets of the labyrinth, King Minos imprisoned him and his son, Icarus. The clever craftsman came up with an ingenious means of escape. As the pair fled to freedom, however, Icarus unintentionally committed an act of hubris and was struck down for his folly.

The myth of Daedalus and Icarus was depicted in Greek paintings, sculptures, and other works of art dating back to the sixth century BCE. However, only a few fragments of the written accounts from ancient

Greece have survived. Fortunately, the Roman poet Ovid preserved this Greek myth in his book *Metamorphoses*, written early in the first century CE.

Dramatis Personae

Minos (MIE-nus) King of Crete

Daedalus (DED-uh-lus) Master craftsman and inventor

Icarus (ICK-uh-rus) Son of Daedalus

Helios (HEE-lee-us) God of the sun

Too Close to the Sun

After Theseus slew the Minotaur and emerged safely from the labyrinth, King Minos of Crete was furious. The king knew that the hero could not have escaped without the help of Daedalus, the ingenious smith who had built the maze and who alone knew its secrets. So Minos locked Daedalus and his young son Icarus in a high tower, while he thought up a suitable punishment. And there father and son remained a long, long time, pining for their freedom.

All through the dreary days and nights, Daedalus stared out the tower window. His cunning mind turned over one scheme of escape after another. There seemed no way to flee the tower, make it safely to the seaside, and cross the waters that were so well guarded by the king's powerful navy. Then, at last, the clever inventor found the answer. The strong hand of Minos might stretch over land and sea, but even the most powerful monarch cannot rule the air.

Quickly, Daedalus set to work. He gathered feathers from the nests of birds that had lodged in the prison tower. He arranged the feathers on a light frame, row upon row, fastening the large ones with fine thread, the smaller with melted wax. Gently, he bent the quills. Gradually, his delicate contraption began to resemble the wings of giant eagles.

While Daedalus worked, Icarus played. Laughing merrily, the young boy tossed feathers in the air and dabbled in the soft wax. Often his childish tricks interfered with his father's work, but Daedalus never scolded. Slowly, the grand design took shape. After much careful labor, the cunning craftsman was ready to fasten the last layer of feathers. He strapped the device to his shoulders and stepped carefully out the window. And there he hung, suspended in the air, beating his marvelous wings.

This relief shows Daedalus and Icarus.

Now Daedalus fixed a smaller set of wings to young Icarus. In a trembling voice, the fond father urged his son to stay close. With tears rolling down his aged cheeks, he told Icarus not to fly too low or the waves would wet his wings, not too high or the sun would melt the wax. Wrapping the child in his arms, he kissed the smooth young brow. Then Daedalus stepped out into the open air and, like a baby bird leaving its nest for the first time, Icarus followed.

Northward over the blue Aegean Sea the pair flew. They passed the islands of Paros and Delos. They passed Samos, center for the worship of Hera, proud queen of the Olympians. As they glided over the coast of that fair isle, a fisherman gazed up in wonder, and a shepherd dropped his staff. A plowman in his fields breathed a prayer, mistaking the great winged creatures for gods.

All this time, young Icarus had heeded his father's warning and kept to the middle air. But as the pair soared through the wide-open skies, the boy began to long for greater heights. In his excitement, he grew wild and careless. Boldly he climbed, higher and higher, as if reaching for heaven itself. Icarus felt the burning anger of Helios the sun god on his back. Ignoring the warning, he climbed still higher. Soon he felt a warm trickle down his shoulders as Helios caused the wax to melt. One by one his feathers loosened and scattered on the breeze. In vain Icarus beat his faltering wings. Crying out to his father, he tumbled from on high and vanished in the deep blue sea.

> Oh! Father, father, as he strove to cry, Down to the sea he tumbled from on high.
>
> ~ Ovid, first century CE

Hearing the boy's cries, Daedalus hurried back. Again and again the father, now a father no more, called out for his son. Then Daedalus saw the feathers scattered over the waves and cursed the cleverness that had led to

Icarus plunges into the sea as Daedalus watches helplessly.

his fatal invention. Circling over the water, he recovered the body of his poor drowned son. He buried Icarus on a nearby island, which he named Icaria in the boy's memory. The sea where Icarus fell has been known ever since as the Icarian Sea.

Daedalus was heartbroken by the loss of his son. Some say that Daedalus flew all the way to Sicily, where he earned riches and fame in the court of the king. Others believe the grieving father found a home in Cumae, in southern Italy. In Cumae, Daedalus built a temple to Apollo. When it was finished, he offered up his wings of feathers and wax as a sad offering to the god of light and science.

Pegasus and Bellerophon

Another myth warning mortals against excessive pride was the tale of Bellerophon (buh-LER-uh-fon) and the winged horse Pegasus. Bellerophon was a hero who performed incredible deeds while riding the magical horse. He killed a fire-breathing monster called the Chimera (kie-MER-uh), and he defeated a race of fierce female warriors known as the Amazons. Bellerophon's victories made him so arrogant that he decided to ride Pegasus to Mount Olympus and join the gods. To punish the man's hubris, Zeus sent a horsefly to sting the flying horse. Bellerophon was thrown to the earth, where he spent the rest of his days lame and blind. Here, the Greek poet Pindar explains how Bellerophon tamed Pegasus with a magical bridle, given to him by the goddess Athena, and then rode the steed to glory.

> As [Bellerophon] slumbered in the darkness ... the daughter herself of Zeus whose spear is the thunderbolt ... brought to him a bridle with golden cheek-pieces ... He seized the marvelous thing that lay beside him [and] eagerly stretched the gentle charmed bridle around [Pegasus's] jaws and caught the winged horse. Mounted on its back and armored in bronze, at once he began to play with weapons. And with Pegasus, from the chilly bosom of the lonely air, he once attacked the Amazons, the female army of archers, and he killed the fire-breathing Chimera ... I shall pass over his death in silence; but Pegasus has found his shelter in the ancient stables of Zeus in Olympus.

Myths of the Trojan War

Some of the most amazing tales in Greek mythology refer to the Trojan War. Here, the Greeks trick the Trojans by presenting a statue of a horse.

The story of the Trojan War is one of the most celebrated of all Greek myths. This epic tale of war covered many subjects of daily life: love, hate, loyalty, betrayal, courage, cowardice, birth, death, triumph, and tragedy. The people of Greece expressed the importance of honor, glory, the perils of angering the gods, and the inescapable nature of fate through their retellings of battles of Troy. The story of the Trojan War was also valued as a turning point in Greek history, the first time Greeks together as one people united in a common cause.

Like many Greek myths, the story of the Trojan War may have been inspired by real events in the distant past. Archaeologists have uncovered part of the ruins of the ancient city of Troy on the western coast of modern-day Turkey. They have found evidence of major military conflicts between the Trojans and invading armies, who may have included the Mycenaean Greeks. For centuries, Greek storytellers passed down the history of those conflicts orally, through their poetry and song. The first written version of the tale appeared in the epic poems the *Iliad* and the *Odyssey*, composed by Homer around the second half of the eighth century BCE. By that time, memories of the Trojan War had been transformed into a complex mythological narrative involving hundreds of superhuman heroes and gods.

According to mythology, the Trojan War began when Paris, prince of Troy, abducted Helen, the beautiful queen of a Greek city-state. To recover Helen and punish the Trojans, the Greeks launched the greatest expedition ever known. For nine years, Greek armies assaulted the walled city of Troy and the surrounding territories. During this long campaign, some of the Olympian gods and goddesses actively supported the Greeks, while others sided with the Trojans. In the tenth year the Greeks came up with a plan for entering Troy and winning the war.

The story of the Trojan War has stirred the imagination of countless writers and artists, from Homer all the way through the present day. Our retelling focuses on the two myths that open and close that epic tale. "The Judgment of Paris" presents the incident that led to the abduction of Helen. "The Trojan Horse" tells of the clever plan that brought about the Greeks' final victory.

The Judgment of Paris

The roots of the Trojan War reach all the way back to a wedding party on the slopes of Mount Pelion. This was no ordinary wedding, but the union of a mortal king and a lovely sea goddess. All the gods and goddesses were invited to celebrate the grand event. All, that is, but one. Eris, goddess of strife, was never invited to such joyful gatherings, because of her talent for stirring up trouble.

Unfortunately, Eris showed up anyway. Just as the guests were raising their cups to toast the happy couple, the goddess strolled in with her eyes flashing and her lips curled in a nasty smile. Calmly, Eris surveyed the immortals who had snubbed her. There was a sudden flash of light as she rolled a shiny orb at their feet. Then—snap! —she vanished. The crowd gathered around the glittering object. It was a golden apple, inscribed with the words "to the fairest."

Dramatis Personae

Eris (ERR-is) Goddess of strife, or conflict

Hera (HER-uh) Queen of the Olympians

Athena (uh-THEE-nuh) Goddess of war and wisdom

Aphrodite (af-ruh-DIE-tee) Goddess of love and beauty

Zeus (zoos) King of the Olympians

Hermes (HER-meez) Messenger of the gods

Paris (PAIR-is) Son of Priam

Priam (PRIE-um) King of Troy

Hecuba (HEH-kyuh-buh) Wife of Priam

Helen (HELL-en) Queen of Sparta; also known as Helen of Troy

Odysseus (oh-DIH-see-us) Famous Greek hero; also known as Ulysses

Sinon (SIE-non) Brave Greek soldier

Laocoön (lay-AH-kuh-wan) Trojan priest

In an instant, three of the Olympian goddesses—Hera, Athena, and Aphrodite—all reached for the lovely apple. A bitter quarrel broke out, with each goddess claiming that she deserved the prize because she was by far the most beautiful. The rivals turned to Zeus, asking him to settle their argument. But the lord of the immortals was no fool. He was not about to take sides in such a delicate matter. Instead, Zeus ordered Hermes to take the three goddesses to a valley near the city of Troy.

There a handsome young shepherd named Paris could decide who was the fairest.

Now, Paris was more than a simple herdsman. In fact, he was a prince, the son of King Priam and Queen Hecuba of Troy. Years earlier, while Hecuba carried her unborn son within her, she had dreamed that she would give birth to a flame that would consume the entire city. The royal couple had been horrified by this evil **omen**. As soon as Paris was born, they reluctantly handed him to a shepherd, ordering the man to kill the ill-fated infant. The shepherd abandoned the little prince on the barren slopes of Mount Ida. When the man returned five days later, however, he found the child alive and well, nursing from a she-bear. Concluding that the gods must have spared the boy's life for some hidden purpose, the shepherd took Paris home and raised him as his own son.

> Come here and decide which is the more excellent beauty of face, and to the fairer give this apple's lovely fruit.
>
> ~ Colluthus, fifth–sixth centuries BCE

So it was that Paris, prince of Troy, stood watching over a flock of sheep when Hermes and the three goddesses appeared before him. The shepherd trembled at the sight of the immortals. But Hermes spoke softly, calming his fears and telling him of the great honor that had been bestowed upon him. In the name of Zeus, the herald commanded Paris to judge which of the golden goddesses was the fairest. Then Hermes rose on his winged sandals and sped away toward the heavens.

Paris gives the lovely Aphrodite the apple, proclaiming her as the most beautiful goddess.

Reassured, the young man began to observe the three divine beauties. Each was perfection itself. How could he ever choose a winner? As he pondered the problem, the goddesses offered an array of wondrous gifts to sway his verdict. Hera promised to make the young man ruler of a rich and powerful kingdom if he would name her the fairest. Athena tempted him with wisdom and glory in battle. Last of all, Aphrodite offered the fairest woman in all the world as his wife. And Paris, judging that love was greater than power or glory, awarded the golden apple to Aphrodite.

The Myth of the Trojan Horse

The judgment of Paris meant disaster for Troy. Shortly after the divine beauty contest, King Priam acknowledged the young shepherd as his son and heir. Paris sailed off to the Greek city-state of Sparta to claim his prize: the most beautiful woman in the world, Helen. With the help of Aphrodite, he persuaded Helen to leave her husband, King Menelaos of Sparta, and elope with him to Troy. That act set off a disastrous war between the Trojans and an invading Greek army.

Year after year, the Trojan War dragged on, with many acts of bravery and turns of fortune on both sides.

Helen's Fault?

Many ancient Greek storytellers denounced Helen for deserting her husband, Menelaos, for Paris, the young prince of Troy. In contrast, Homer presented her as a sympathetic character who, like all mortals, was simply a tool of the gods. In this scene from Homer's Iliad, Helen meets King Priam and his counselors on the walls of Troy.

> Watching Helen as she climbed the stair [the counselors] said to one another: "We cannot rage at her, it is no wonder that Trojans and [Greeks] under arms should for so long have borne the pains of war for one like this. Unearthliness. A goddess the woman is to look at." ... To Helen Priam called out: "Come here, dear child, sit here beside me ... You are not to blame, I hold the gods to blame for bringing on this war against the [Greeks] to our sorrow ... And the great beauty, Helen, replied: "Revere you as I do, I dread you, too, dear father. Painful death would have been sweeter for me, on that day I joined your son, and left my bridal chamber, my brothers, my grown child, my childhood friends! But no death came, though I have pined and wept.

Still, the people of Troy held out inside their walled city. The Greeks, weary of bloodshed and longing for home, began to despair of ever subduing their enemy.

Then Athena, who hated the Trojans because Paris had judged her less beautiful than Aphrodite, whispered a plan to the wily Greek chieftain Odysseus. Under his direction, the Greeks built a huge wooden horse with a great hollow belly. One side of the horse held a cunningly concealed door. On the other side was an inscription: for their return home, the Greeks dedicate this thanks-offering to Athena.

> Two serpents swam through the sea from the neighboring islands and devoured the sons of Laocoön.
>
> ~ Apollodorus, second century BCE

When night fell, Odysseus and fifty armed warriors climbed into the belly of the horse. The rest of the Greeks burned their tents, boarded their ships, and sailed to the far side of a nearby island. Only one man remained. This was a brave soldier named Sinon, who had volunteered to stay behind and allow himself to be captured.

The next morning the Trojans awoke to find the enemy camp deserted and the colossal fleet gone. Throwing open their gates, they poured out of the city to rejoice in their victory and marvel at the giant horse. Some of the Trojans wanted to bring the image inside the city as a trophy. Others, distrusting the monstrous beast, wanted to light a bonfire beneath it. As the two sides argued, a shout arose and a group of shepherds dragged in the Greek soldier Sinon. With much trembling and rolling of eyes, the captive told his false tale. After a quarrel with Odysseus, Sinon said bitterly, he had been left behind to die. As for the wooden horse, that was an offering to Athena, made by his former comrades to ensure favorable winds on their return journey. Then Sinon confided a great secret. The Greeks had purposely made the horse too big to pass through the gates of Troy. For if the Trojans took the sacred image into their city, they would gain mastery over all their enemies.

Hearing Sinon's tale, the Trojans clamored to bring in the wondrous horse. Only the wise priest Laocoön still urged caution. The priest hurled his spear at the wooden beast. He warned his countrymen to beware of gifts from the treacherous Greeks. But as Laocoön spoke, Athena grew angry at his interference. The goddess caused two immense serpents to rise from the sea. Hissing and sputtering flames, the monsters slithered swiftly across the beach. They wrapped their giant coils around Laocoön and his two young sons and choked them to death.

Now fear and amazement seized the Trojans. Many shouted that Athena had sent the serpents to punish the priest for dishonoring her sacred image. Quickly, men fastened wheels to the horse's feet and tied ropes around its flanks. Eagerly they pried stones from the city walls to enlarge the gates. Then a throng of the strongest Trojans hauled the unwieldy steed through the gates to a place of honor outside Athena's temple.

Long and loud were the celebrations on that festive occasion. It was the middle of the night before the Trojans finally retired, worn out with wine and merriment. As they slept, the traitor Sinon lit a beacon fire to guide

A bust of the beautiful woman, Helen of Troy

the Greek fleet back to shore. He knocked on the door of the wooden horse to summon the hidden warriors. Silently the soldiers slid down a rope to the street. They unbarred the gates of Troy and admitted their army. Then, marching through the city, the Greeks began to enter the houses and slaughter the Trojans in their beds.

Trumpets rang out, calling the men of Troy to repel the foe. The clash of arms mingled with loud laments, and the streets flowed with blood. A crackling fire, borne by the wind, consumed homes, temples, and palaces. By the break of day, all but a few of the Trojan men had been slain, and the women and children were dead or taken captive.

But what happened to Helen, whose divine beauty had caused the horrible war? She was reunited with Menelaos, the husband she had never ceased to love. For though Aphrodite had bewitched her into betraying him for another, Helen's true feelings had never changed. The couple returned to Sparta and lived together happily for many years. Finally, when they died, the gods took them to the Elysian Fields, where they spend eternity by one another's side.

GLOSSARY

ambrosia The food of the Greek gods, which had the power to give immortality to mortals.

archaeologists Scientists who study the physical remains of past cultures to learn about human life and activity.

city-states Independent states that were made up of a city and its surrounding territory.

deities Gods, goddesses, and other divine beings.

epic A long, narrative poem celebrating the deeds of legendary or historical beings.

genealogy A record of the descent of individuals from their ancestors.

hubris Excessive pride or arrogance; in ancient Greece, hubris was also a term that referred to the act of taking pleasure in insulting or dishonoring a person.

Macedonia An ancient kingdom on the Balkan Peninsula, centered in a plain north of Mount Olympus, which was ruled by Philip II and his son Alexander the Great.

Minoan Relating to the people or culture of ancient Crete, beginning around 3000 BCE.

minstrels Entertainers who traveled from place to place, playing music, singing verses, and reciting poetry.

Mycenaean Relating to the people or culture of Mycenae, the ancient city that reached its height around 1400 BCE and was the center of the first great civilization of mainland Greece.

mythology The whole body of myths belonging to a people.

myths Traditional stories about gods and other divine and sometimes mortal beings, which were developed by ancient cultures to explain the mysteries of the physical and spiritual worlds.

nectar The sweet drink of the Olympian gods.

nymphs Fairylike beings who were believed to dwell in rivers, pools, trees, and mountains.

omen An occurrence that is believed to be a sign of good or bad luck to come.

Panhellenic Relating to all of Greece or all the Greek people.

patron Deity a god or goddess adopted by a polis as its special protector.

polis One of the city-states of ancient Greece; the plural is poleis.

polytheists People who believe in more than one god.

pomegranate A thick-skinned, reddish fruit with many tart seeds.

prophecy A prediction of something to come.

Tartarus A deep, sunless region in the lowest part of the underworld.

tribute A payment given by one ruler or country to another as a sign of respect and submission.

tyrants Rulers who took over city-states and established dynasties (hereditary ruling families).

BIOGRAPHICAL DICTIONARY OF GREEK WRITERS

The following are brief biographies of the ancient Greek poets, playwrights, historians, and other writers mentioned in this book.

Aeschylus (ESS-kuh-lus) 525–456 BCE
The playwright Aeschylus is often called the father of Greek tragedy. He is believed to have written about ninety plays, but only seven have survived. His best-known plays were tragedies, or serious dramas describing a conflict between the main character and a larger force such as fate. Aeschylus's tragedies included *Prometheus Bound*, the story of the Titan honored as the champion of humankind, and *Agamemnon*, the tale of a Greek hero's disastrous return from the Trojan War.

Apollodorus around second century BCE
The Greek scholar Apollodorus is most famous for his *Chronicle*, a history of Greece from the legendary fall of Troy in the eleventh century BCE to 144 BCE. He also wrote several works on grammar and mythology.

Colluthus fifth–sixth centuries BCE
Colluthus of Lycopolis was a Greek poet known for his one surviving work, *The Rape of Helen*. This epic poem recounts the events leading up to the Trojan War, from

the Judgment of Paris to the “rape,” or abduction, of Helen from Sparta.

Diodorus Siculus around 90–21 BCE
This Greek historian wrote the *Bibliotheca Historica*, or *Library of History*, a forty-volume work claiming to cover the history of the entire world from the creation through the early years of the Roman Empire. Diodorus’s ambitious work was drawn from his extensive travels and from the writings of earlier historians.

Hesiod eighth century BCE
The poet Hesiod is known mainly for two long poems, *Theogony*, or *Genealogy of the Gods*, and *Works and Days*. *Theogony* draws on earlier traditional tales to tell the story of the creation of the world and the birth of the gods. *Works and Days* offers advice on moral living and the importance of honest work. It is the first known didactic poem, which means that it was intended to be educational or instructive rather than simply entertaining.

Homer ninth–eighth centuries BCE
Homer is traditionally considered the composer of the two most important epic poems from ancient Greece, the *Iliad* and the *Odyssey*. The *Iliad* is set in the last year of the Trojan War, and the *Odyssey* describes the long homeward journey of the heroic Greek warrior Odysseus. Some scholars believe that one or both of the epics may actually be collections of works by several different poets.

Pindar around 522–438 BCE
Pindar is often called Greece's greatest writer of lyric poetry, or songlike poems meant to be chanted or sung. Most of his surviving poems were composed in honor of the victors at the Olympian Games and other national festivals.

Plato around 428–348 BCE
The Greek philosopher Plato is considered one of the most important and influential thinkers of the Western world. He founded one of the first universities, the Academy in Athens. Plato wrote a series of dialogues, which presented philosophical ideas in the form of conversations between two or more people. His best-known work was *The Republic*, a dialogue exploring the meaning and value of justice.

Plutarch (PLOO-tark) around 46–120 CE
The writer Plutarch is best known for his *Parallel Lives*, also known as *Plutarch's Lives*, a series of biographies comparing the lives of famous Greeks and Romans. Along with well-researched historical information, the biographies explored the influence of the subjects' characters on their lives and destinies. Plutarch also wrote on such topics as morality, religion, and philosophy.

FURTHER INFORMATION

Books

Ashworth, Leon. *Gods and Goddesses of Ancient Greece.* North Mankato, MN: Smart Apple Media, 2003.

Bolton, Lesley. *The Everything Classical Mythology Book.* Avon, MA: Adams Media, 2002.

Daly, Kathleen N. *Greek and Roman Mythology A to Z.* Revised edition. New York: Facts on File, 2004.

Evslin, Bernard. *Heroes, Gods and Monsters of the Greek Myths.* New York: Four Winds Press, 1999.

Fagles, Robert, trans. *The Iliad.* New York: Penguin Classics, 1998.

Freeman, Philip. Oh My Gods: *A Modern Retelling of Greek and Roman Myths.* New York: Simon & Schuster, 2013.

Hamilton, Edith. *Mythology: Timeless Tales of Gods and Heroes.* New York: Grand Central Publishing, 2011.

López-Ruiz, Carolina. *Gods, Heroes, and Monsters: A Sourcebook of Greek, Roman, and Near Eastern Myths in Translation.* New York: Oxford University Press, 2013.

Morales, Helen. *Classical Mythology: A Very Short Introduction.* New York, Oxford University Press, 2007.

Waterfield, Robin and Kathryn Waterfield. *The Greek Myths.* New York: Quercus, 2012.

Websites

Encyclopedia Mythica

www.pantheon.org/areas/mythology/europe/greek/articles.html

This online encyclopedia contains hundreds of articles on the gods, goddesses, heroes, and legendary creatures of ancient Greece.

Greek Mythology, Ancient History

www.history.com/topics/ancient-history/greek-mythology

Watch a video about the role of gods and goddesses in Ancient Greek society, learn about the sources of Greek myths, and find out about Olympians, heroes, and monsters.

Greek Mythology, Archeological Excavations in Greece

greekarchaeology.osu.edu/arch-edu/mythology

This website, created by Ohio State University, delves deeper into the question "what is myth?" and offers exploration into different areas in Greece. Find out more about myths and archeological studies that OSU is conducting on Isthmia.

Windows to the Universe, World Mythology

www.windows2universe.org/mythology/worldmap_new.html

Created by the University of Michigan, this excellent site gives visitors a choice of information presented at beginning, intermediate, or advanced levels. Click on the word "Greek" on the world map for information and art relating to the Greek gods and heroes.

World Myths and Legends in Art

www.artsmia.org/world-myths/artbyculture/greek.html

The Minneapolis Institute of Arts presents this collection of works of art inspired by Greek and Roman myths. The site includes images of ancient and modern-day paintings and sculptures, along with summaries of the myths, background information on culture, and discussion questions.

SELECTED BIBLIOGRAPHY

Avery, Catherine B., ed. *The New Century Handbook of Greek Mythology and Legend*. New York: Appleton-Century-Crofts, 1972.

Bulfinch, Thomas. *The Golden Age of Myth and Legend*. Hertfordshire, England: Wordsworth Reference, 1993.

Buxton, Richard. *The Complete World of Greek Mythology*. London: Thames and Hudson, 2004.

Cotterell, Arthur. *Classical Mythology*. New York: Lorenz Books, 2000.

Diodorus Siculus. *Library of History. Vol. 3.* Translated by C. H. Oldfather. Cambridge, MA: Harvard University Press, 1985.

Field, D. M. *Greek and Roman Mythology*. New York: Chartwell Books, 1977.

Hesiod. *Theogony*. Translated by Norman O. Brown. Indianapolis: Bobbs-Merrill, 1953.

———. *Works and Days and Theogony*. Translated by Stanley Lombardo. Indianapolis, IN: Hackett Publishing, 1993.

Homer. *Iliad*. Translated by Robert Fitzgerald. Garden City, NY: Doubleday, 1974.

———. *Odyssey*. Translated by Robert Fitzgerald. Garden City, NY: Doubleday, 1961.

Kokkinou, Sophia. *Greek Mythology*. Athens, Greece: Intercarta, 1989.

Murray, Alexander S. *Manual of Mythology*. Edited by William H. Klapp. New York: Tudor, 1935.

Schmidt, Joel. *Larousse Greek and Roman Mythology*. Edited by Dr. Seth Benardete. New York: McGraw-Hill, 1980.

Souli, Sofia A. *Greek Mythology*. Ilioupoli, Greece: Editions Michalis Toubis, 1995.

Summers, Kirk. *Greek and Roman Mythology*. Dubuque, IA: Kendall/Hunt Publishing, 2003.

Wright, John Henry, ed. *Masterpieces in Greek Literature*. Freeport, NY: Books for Libraries, 1970.

QUOTATION CITATIONS

Quoted passages in sidebars come from the following sources:

"How Aphrodite Was Born," page 33, from Hesiod, *Theogony*, translated by Norman O. Brown (New York: Bobbs-Merrill Company, 1953).

"Sacrificing the Bones," page 41, from Hesiod, *Works and Days and Theogony*, translated by Stanley Lombardo (Indianapolis, IN: Hackett, 1993).

"The Afterlife of the Greeks," page 48, from Plato, *Gorgias*, translated by Benjamin Jowett, at www.ancienttexts.org/library/greek/plato/gorgias.html

"Demeter's Temple," page 52, from the *Homeric Hymn to Demeter*, translated by Hugh G. Evelyn-White, at www.sacred-texts.com/cla/demeter.htm

"The Strength of Hercules," page 59, from *Plutarch's Lives: Theseus*, translated by John Dryden, at classics.mit.edu/Plutarch/theseus.html

"How the Minotaur Came to Be," page 63, from Diodorus Siculus, *Library of History, Vol. 3*, translated by C. H. Oldfather (Cambridge, MA: Harvard University Press, 1985).

"Pegasus and Bellerophon," page 71, from Pindar, *Odes*, "Olympian XIII," at The Perseus Digital Library, translated by Basil L. Gildersleeve and Anne Mahoney, at www.perseus.tufts.edu

"Helen's Fault?," page 78, from Homer, The *Iliad*, translated by Robert Fitzgerald (Garden City, NY: Doubleday, 1974).

INDEX